Original title:
Vine Lines

Copyright © 2025 Creative Arts Management OÜ
All rights reserved.

Author: Vivienne Beaumont
ISBN HARDBACK: 978-1-80566-602-8
ISBN PAPERBACK: 978-1-80566-887-9

Whimsical Cling

A grape took a leap, oh what a sight,
It flopped on a leaf, with all its might.
"Hello, my dear friend, mind the fall!"
The leaf just chuckled, "Not worried at all!"

The sun winks down, glossy skin shines,
The air whispers sweetly, laced with good times.
With every twist, it dangles and sways,
In a playful dance, it giggles and plays.

Dance of the Canopy

In shadows they sway, a jolly parade,
Each leaf a dancer, in sunlight they played.
The branches all jostle, a lively affair,
While bugs start to boogie, without any care.

A squirrel joins in, with a dash and a twirl,
He trips on a acorn, gives nature a whirl.
No rhythm too crazy, too wild, or too odd,
In the great arching leaves, nature's a god.

Sinuous Song

A creeping surprise on the garden wall,
With twists and with turns, it beckons us all.
"Come dance on my edges, let's sway in the breeze,"
It whispers softly, rustling with ease.

The sun blinks and giggles, in goldens and greens,
As shadows play tricks in the afternoon scenes.
The creatures join in, from bug to bird,
A symphony rises, the joy is absurd.

The Embrace of Green

In an emerald hug, all tangled and tight,
The leaves share a secret, they whisper goodnight.
"Stay close, little buddy, let's weather this storm,"
They giggle and chuckle, a quirky warm charm.

From roots to the sky, a mischievous crew,
With laughter that echoes, and a playful view.
Each twist and each turn tells a story unseen,
In the heart of the garden, where fun's evergreen.

Shadows and Sunshine

In the garden, a gnome grins wide,
Tripping over roots, he almost cried.
Sunshine tickles his pointy hat,
He scolds the squirrels for being brat.

Dandelions dance with the breeze,
While bees do the polka, with such ease.
Giggling tulips in hot pursuit,
Throwing shade at the cantankerous fruit.

The sun winks at a lazy cat,
Who dreams of catching a flying rat.
Rabbits giggle, making a scene,
Wishing for carrots in fields of green.

Whispers in the Wilderness

A raccoon wearing a tiny hat,
Chasing fireflies, oh, imagine that!
Whispers float through the trees at night,
As owls share gossip, what a delight.

Bears breakdance by the old oak tree,
While deer sip tea, quite relaxed, you see.
The wind tells tales of an old racquet,
As frogs croak croons, none could hack it.

Hoots and toots fill the moonlit air,
Echoes of laughter everywhere.
Squirrels with nutty puns in store,
Keep everyone giggling forevermore.

Clusters of Color

A patchwork quilt of blooms unfolds,
Tulips chat, gossip, and both are bold.
Roses wear hats, just for the show,
While daisies tumble, putting on a glow.

Colors clash like clowns on parade,
With butterflies dancing, never afraid.
Lavender giggles, tickled by air,
Chasing the sun without a care.

Petunias paint the town so bright,
While sunflowers flex in morning light.
Clusters of petals, what a sight to see,
In a world where flowers dance wild and free.

Petals of Possibility

In a world where petals know how to chat,
Each one a dream or a friendly spat.
Butterflies wager on whose will fly,
While daisies squeal, 'Oh me, oh my!'

A quirky tulip claims she's the best,
As snippy daisies put her to the test.
Posies tumble, doing their stuff,
As they ponder, 'Is this enough?'

Colors giggle, weaving tales of cheer,
All the blooms come together here.
Creating a ruckus, a riot of hue,
Petals of fun, for me and for you.

Unraveled Tales of Nature's Embrace

In the garden, sunlight gleams,
Where green things dance, or so it seems.
A snail races a tiny bee,
And both declare, "You know it's me!"

The tulips gossip, tipsy and bright,
While daisies giggle, pure delight.
A worm in a suit, quite dapper and grand,
Says, "I'm off to the ball, come lend me a hand!"

Spirals of Hope in Earth's Canvas

A twisty path of tangled cheer,
Where carrots hide, in soil they steer.
Radishes blush with laughter so bold,
They whisper secrets, their stories told!

The sunflowers nod in goofy refrain,
Chasing shadows in the summer rain.
A ladybug spins tales of the breeze,
Sipping nectar with utmost ease.

Knotted Emotions of Growth and Change

In a pot, a sprout sings low,
"I'm not a weed, just let me grow!"
A cactus jokes, prickly and wise,
"Come hug me close, but mind your size!"

Leaves swap tales of tangled plans,
Of wild winds and cozy span.
While clovers chuckle at fate's silly game,
With every twist, they're never the same!

The Garden's Silent Confessions

In shadows deep where shadows dwell,
The herbs have secrets, can you tell?
Basil sings of a love so sweet,
While mint whispers, "Life's a treat!"

The thyme complains, "I'm always late,"
Thistles poke fun at their fate.
In blooms so bright, joy feels like magic,
With each petal tossed, life's tragic—we laugh it!

Winding Voyage

A twisty path, with laughs in tow,
We stumble forth, high and low.
Beneath the leaves, a hidden trip,
We giggle loud, then take a dip.

Oh what a dance, we spin around,
With every turn, new sights abound.
Like tangled yarn, we spin and twirl,
In this wild maze, let laughter whirl.

Nebulous Horizons

In cloudy realms where whims reside,
We steer our boats, on giggles ride.
A hiccup here, a laugh out there,
Our jokes float high, with nary a care.

The sun peeks through, with cheeky glee,
As we chase dreams, like bumblebees.
With every joke, the clouds disband,
In this bright space, we've got it planned.

Tapestry of Twists

A woven tale, with threads of cheer,
Laughter flies, from ear to ear.
Every loop holds a goofy jest,
In tangled hues, we find our zest.

With colors bright, and pokes of fun,
We weave our dream, till day is done.
The craft of joy, in stitches tight,
Our hearts are light, in this warm light.

The Grasp of Growth

With silly sprouts and roots of giggle,
We dance around, and do a wiggle.
A sprout pokes up with a wink and grin,
Saying, 'Join me, let the fun begin!'

The garden's wild with laughter's sound,
In every nook, joy's always found.
From tiny seeds, our smiles take flight,
Together we bloom, so bold and bright.

Echoes of Green

In gardens where the weeds all cheer,
The plants plot jokes that we can't hear.
A daisy winks at a passing bee,
While the sun plays tricks on a thirsty tree.

Each leaf a comedian, leaves no doubt,
Tickling the branches, they laugh out loud.
With every gust, they dance in grace,
Turning the garden to a funny place.

The Clutch of Nature

A squirrel steals acorns from under your nose,
While flowers gossip in froggy prose.
The earthworms underground tell silly tales,
Of one that tried swimming, but ended up frail.

The sunbeam sneezes, the clouds burst in glee,
As if that's their plan, to make bright rain free.
Nature's clutch, with humor so thick,
Leaves us chuckling, just like a trick.

Spirals of Serenity

The ivy creeps up, a mischievous sprout,
Hiding in places we'd never scout.
Cacti giggle, with prickly jests,
As they welcome guests with humorous quests.

Branches twist round, they play tag in the air,
Leaves sharing secrets, without any care.
Serenity's spiral is a lighthearted jest,
Laughter's the fruit that nature behests.

Hidden Journeys

Down the path where colors collide,
A snail tells tales of his slow, calm ride.
The mushrooms giggle in their funny hats,
While bees buzz around, doing little chats.

In the shallow streams, where the minnows play,
Fish swim in circles, always making hay.
Hidden journeys, each twist and bend,
Nature's punchlines, a humorous blend.

Beneath a Canopy

Under leaves where shadows play,
Squirrels dance in silly fray.
Laughter drips from boughs above,
Nature's jest, a push and shove.

Funny hats on weary heads,
Birds gossip, sharing spreads.
A bumblebee in striped attire,
Buzzes jokes to lift us higher.

Pine cones drop like comets bold,
Nuts exchanged like gifts of gold.
The breeze tickles, a prankster quick,
Trees giggle, it's all quite slick.

Under this lofty, leafy scene,
Every twig becomes a queen.
We're guests at a leafy jest,
In the forest, we are blessed!

Climbing Echoes

Up the trunks, the antics grow,
Lizards leap in limbo flow.
Branches creak, a comic tune,
As raccoons tap dance to the moon.

Echoes bounce from tree to tree,
Each giggle a mystery.
Squirrels trade their acorn bling,
While frogs croak, as if to sing.

Tangled limbs in laughter thread,
Whispers swirl above our heads.
Mice in suits at a gala feast,
A wild party, not the least!

Oh, the stories they could share,
Of woodland pranks, and furry flair.
Let's climb high where giggles ring,
In the echo of each spring!

Roots of Reflection

Beneath the soil where secrets dwell,
Worms are chatting, casting spells.
With tiny hats and laughter bright,
They plan their pranks by starlight.

Nuts debating, who's the best,
Mushrooms as the honored guest.
Old oak chuckles, wisdom wide,
Sharing tales with roots as guides.

Sticky sap and a riddle shared,
Bugs convene, no one scared.
A ladybug tells a tall tale,
While laughing leaves begin to pale.

Reflections dance in muddy pools,
Frogs wear crowns made of jewels.
Life's a game, they all agree,
In nature's heart, so wild and free!

Nature's Embrace

In the thicket, giggles rise,
Flowers chuckle, surprise, surprise!
Bouncing grasses, wit so sly,
Tickle toes as breezes sigh.

A hedgehog dons a dapper coat,
As beetles dance and take a vote.
"Who's the best?" they chirp and shout,
In the fun, there is no doubt.

Each petal wears a smiling face,
While honeybees quicken their pace.
A mischief here, a joke or two,
In this realm of greenish hue.

Nature's spirit, light and gay,
Spreading laughter every day.
Join the ruckus, join the fun,
In this embrace, we all are one!

The Lattice of Life

In a garden plot so bright,
Plants dance with pure delight.
Their twirls are quite the sight,
A subtle, leafy kite.

A tomato with a hat,
Said, "Look at me, so sprat!"
While the peas in a chat,
Claim that they're all that.

The beans move with a jig,
Just look at that tall twig!
Laughing near a big fig,
They all fit like a gig.

With trellises so fine,
Each twist creates a line.
A nature's grand design,
Where giggles intertwine.

Woven Whispers

In tangled tales of green,
A whisper can be seen.
A fern with dress so keen,
Mocks how bright grass has been.

A gnome with jokes to tell,
Stands guard near a dry well.
While the daisies yell,
"Hear the stories we sell!"

Entwined but full of glee,
"Do you think we'll be free?"
Said the ivy on a spree,
"We'll climb each ancient tree!"

As laughter starts to rise,
And sunlight paints the skies,
Nature spins and ties,
In this weave of surprise.

Serpentines of Stillness

In curves that twist and twine,
Beneath a sun that shines.
The garden's peace aligns,
With laughter in designs.

The snail wearing a shoe,
Glides by with quite the view.
Said, "Take it nice and slow,
Or you might miss the show!"

A neighbor's cat, so spry,
Caught perched up high, oh my!
Hoping for a butterfly,
Or at least a passing fly.

From shadows soft and deep,
To bright blooms, secrets keep.
Each twist a giggle heap,
As nature starts to creep.

Heartstrings in Bloom

A flower with a grin,
Swayed gently in the wind.
"Hey you, come join the fun,
Let's shine like the sun!"

The daisies link up tight,
Throwing a color fight.
Petal battles take flight,
What a glorious sight!

A gopher pops his head,
With mischief all widespread.
"Who needs a cozy bed?
This show is enough said!"

As blooms all intertwine,
Heartstrings begin to shine.
With joy, they all align,
In a dance so divine.

Intertwined Paths of Growth

In the garden, sprouts do dance,
Twisting through a leafy trance.
Roots are tangled, jokes abound,
Laughter echoes underground.

Little buds with faces bright,
Crack a smile in morning light.
With every twist, they share a tale,
Of blooming dreams that never pale.

Embracing the Unsung Flora

Oh, the blooms that often hide,
Dressed in green, not one with pride.
Tickled petals, such a sight,
Whisper secrets in the night.

In the shade, they plot their schemes,
Growing wild on sunshine dreams.
Amid the grass, they spill their tea,
"Drink it up, it's good," says me!

Echoes of an Untamed Forest

Amidst the trees, the critters play,
In branches high, they joke all day.
Squirrels gossip, birds all chirp,
In this place, all worries slurp.

Leaves laugh softly in the breeze,
Nature's humor brings us ease.
In every nook, a creature peeks,
With open hearts and joyous squeaks.

Weaving Life's Serpentine Stories

Twisting tales in every thread,
Where laughter blooms and worries shed.
Bouncing back from every bend,
Life's a joke that has no end.

From roots that dig to stars that shine,
We weave our dreams with every line.
So come, my friend, and join the ride,
In this wild dance, let's find our stride.

Climbing Secrets

In secret spots where twiggy folks,
Clamber high to crack a joke.
A flower creeps and starts to tease,
"You need more style, oh, climb with ease!"

With silly hats and wobbly shoes,
They swing from branches, pick and choose.
A squirrel snickers, joins the fuss,
'It's all a game! Oh, climb with us!'

The leaves start giggling, twitch and sway,
'Who knew our friends could dance this way?'
Amidst the bark and pretty sights,
The laughter echoes through the nights!

So if you hear a rustle, run,
It's just the trees having some fun.
Join the climb, but take good care,
For sticky sap can tangle hair!

Nature's Tapestry

Beautiful threads in emerald lace,
Stitching smiles on every face.
The daisies giggle in the breeze,
Tickling each other, 'Oh, do you please?'

A butterfly slips, oh what a sight!
Wings like puns take off in flight.
They sway and shimmer, paint the ground,
Nature's jesters all around!

A robin jokes with worms in tow,
'What's the secret to a good throw?'
While crickets chirp with a sharp wit,
'Our concert starts at half-past it!'

So come and see this colorful blend,
Where every leaf has a joke to send.
In nature's quilt, let laughter bloom,
A tapestry brightens every room!

Twisting Through Dreams

In the garden of sleep, where shadows meet,
A snail in shades leaves tiny feet.
He glides with grace, "Catch me if you can!"
While dreaming daisies cheer, "Oh, what a plan!"

A hedgehog rolls with a giggly spin,
"Do you think I'm ready? Where do I begin?"
Twists and turns in this friendly race,
"Faster, faster! Let's quicken the pace!"

The moonlight chuckles, dances above,
"It's all a joke, wrapped in love!"
In this playful maze where laughter sways,
Chasing dreams in silly ways.

The night smiles wide, so soft and bright,
Whispering secrets, sprouting delight.
Join the chase in this cosmic game,
For in waking hours, we're never the same!

The Dance of Leaves

Leaves twirl around in a frisky show,
Whispering secrets in the wind's blow.
They giggle and hop, from branch to ground,
In this merry game, laughter resounds.

With autumn's brush, a crazy mix,
Colors collide—oh, what a fix!
They spin like tops in joy's parade,
Flaunting dreams that never fade.

A squirrel leaps in a nutty seminar,
Trying to teach a chipmunk guitar.
With every strum, they break into song,
Nature joins in, it feels so strong!

So watch the leaves in their light-hearted spree,
In every shimmer, a quirky decree.
Join the dance, get lost in delight,
For life's a waltz on a sunny night!

Curls of Color

In a garden, twists and bends,
Colorful antics, nature sends.
A green grape juggles, oh so bold,
While pickles laugh, their tales retold.

Ribbons of laughter dress the ground,
Bouncing bugs with jokes abound.
A tomato yells, 'I'm ripe and sassy!'
While carrots cringe, feeling quite classy.

A twisty turn, a pirouette,
The sun's bright wink we can't forget.
Squash goes goofy, doing a spin,
While peppers ponder what's next akin.

In this patch, fun never stops,
Hilarity hops and joy flips, hops.
With curls of color, nature sings,
Funny moments, what joy it brings!

Threads of Nature

In the weave of leaves, stories twine,
Laughter echoes, oh how they shine!
A spider spins a web of rhyme,
Teasing ants, 'You're late this time!'

A worm with style, not just a bug,
Wears a jacket, snug as a hug.
The daisies dance in silly glee,
Telling tales of what will be.

The breeze tosses jokes, wild and free,
Tickling flowers with glee, oh me!
A bee buzzes in, mouthful of fun,
'Pollinate? Nah, I'm off to run!'

Brown branches laugh with stories grand,
While clouds giggle, high above the land.
Nature threads its humor tight,
In this tapestry, pure delight.

Weaving the Wild

In the forest, threads entwine,
Squirrels crack jokes, feeling fine.
A raccoon winks, his munchy snack,
Giggling softly in the back.

Twisting grasses, swaying tall,
Invite each critter to the ball.
A fox with flair, and a bunny's hop,
Makes the woodland stop and bop!

Underneath the mushroom dome,
Fungi ponder their grand poem.
A chorus of croaks joins the mix,
While shadows twist with funny tricks.

Weaving the wild, in nature's style,
Where laughter echoes, mile after mile.
From tree to tree, in merry play,
Every moment's a bright bouquet!

The Quiet Ascent

Up the hill where the whispers creep,
Laughter stirs from dreams in sleep.
A dandelion, bold and bright,
Shouts, 'Stay with me, don't take flight!'

The climb is steep, the jokes unfold,
A berry giggles, feeling bold.
An acorn cracks a randomized pun,
'Why not climb? It's all just fun!'

With every step, chuckles trail,
Nature's secrets, humorous and pale.
A breeze named Chuckle leads the way,
Tickling blossoms at play all day.

The quiet ascent, a merry spree,
Where giggles hide among the trees.
As we reach the peak, let's laugh and cheer,
In this whimsical world, joy is near!

Tendrils of Whispered Secrets

In the garden, secrets grow,
Whispers from the flowers flow.
The daisies giggle, tulips tease,
Bending low with playful ease.

A gnome overheard a silly tale,
Of a snail who dreamed to sail.
He donned a hat of leafy greens,
And rode a frog, or so it seems!

The sun peeks in, its rays a laugh,
Tickling petals in the path.
Butterflies join the grand parade,
While ladybugs serenade!

So tread lightly in this plot,
For fun awaits in every spot.
The garden's secrets, light and spry,
A hidden world where giggles lie.

Green Threads of Heartfelt Connection

In the park, a new bench glows,
Where friendship blooms as laughter flows.
Squirrels gossip, chattering loud,
About a cat that's far too proud.

Beneath the leaves, a picnic lies,
Filled with sandwiches and surprise.
"Is that a bug?" a voice did squeak,
But laughter wins, and fears grow sleek.

A game of tag breaks out and flies,
With roots beneath, they leap and rise.
The grass applauds with every fall,
While daisies dance and cheer them all.

So grab a friend, and take a seat,
Let joy be found in every beat.
Connection sprouts beneath the sun,
In laughter shared, we all are one.

Roots Beneath the Surface

A tale unfolds beneath the soil,
Where whispers bubble, laughter boils.
Roots play hide and seek all day,
As ants march by in grand display.

"I'll bet a nut I'm faster," brags,
Said the root to those pulling jags.
But a worm winks and gives a twist,
"I'll teach you all, you can't resist!"

With tangled tales and silly spins,
Each root debates who always wins.
In darkened depths, the humor's bright,
As snickers sprout in endless flight.

So while you think what lies above,
Remember roots that laugh and love.
It's down below where fun takes hold,
A secret world, joyful and bold.

Twisted Journeys of the Soul

Life's a path with turns and bends,
Where laughter mingles with good friends.
A garden party, tangled fun,
Underneath the laughing sun.

With every twist, a story grows,
Of lost socks and hidden toes.
A dizzy dance around the pot,
Drunk on cookies, lost the plot!

Going left when right was true,
A flower in a shoe, oh boo!
Yet every step leads to surprise,
In the garden of joyful sighs.

So wander on, don't take the lane,
Embrace the chaos, feel the gain.
For in the twists of life's great stroll,
You'll find the joys that feed the soul.

Lush Labyrinths

In a garden maze I roam,
Where plants have claimed their home.
Twisting paths and leafy cheer,
I get lost with a grin ear to ear.

The tomatoes try to sneak a chat,
While cucumbers cling, imagine that!
Beneath the leaves, a gnome appears,
With a wink, he spreads the cheers.

Rabbits hop, a sneaky dance,
While carrots giggle at their chance.
The sun sets low, the shadows play,
In this green world, I must stay.

I stumble through this leafy spree,
Found my hat atop a tree.
With each step, a silly slip,
In lush labyrinths, I take a trip.

The Arc of Growth

From seed to sprout, what a sight,
Watching greens, a pure delight.
A beanpole stands, proud and tall,
While nearby cabbages start to sprawl.

Carrots wiggle in the soil,
Chasing worms with cheeky toil.
Zucchini flexes, feeling grand,
While pumpkins dream of ice cream stands.

Each stalk and leaf, a tale to tell,
In this sunny garden, all is well.
I chat with flowers, they chat back,
In the rhythm of this leafy track.

With every bloom, the laughter grows,
In the arc of life, anything goes!
So let's toast to greens, of every hue,
In the garden's heart, we're never blue.

Cradled in Hues

In the patch, a rainbow stands,
Each color sprout, with eager hands.
The peppers giggle, bright and bold,
While eggplants wear their royal gold.

Carrots dig in, a splash of orange,
Radishes peek, feeling so strange.
Broccoli heads nod in surprise,
As tiny beets play hide and guise.

In this vibrant, playful sprawl,
Nature's laughter, heard by all.
With petals dancing in the air,
Every hue whispers to beware.

For in this chaos, joy is found,
In every twist, life spins around.
Cradled in hues, we swirl and sway,
In a garden filled with play.

Silken Footprints

Through the leaves, I tiptoe light,
Making paths in the soft twilight.
The caterpillars cheer me on,
As I shimmy past the sleepy dawn.

A spider spins her silky webs,
While I dodge the swinging ebb.
"Watch your step!" the daisies shout,
As I dance and twirl about.

Each footprint leaves a funny trace,
In this garden, a wacky race.
With laughing birds that sing and chirp,
I take a plunge, an awkward slurp.

Through tangled greens, I hop and glide,
Every inch, a merry ride.
With silken threads that wrap around,
In this crazy joy, I'm tightly bound.

Enigmatic Growth

In a garden where gnomes play,
A mystery grows day by day.
Twisting and turning with flair,
Plants gossip in the warm air.

With leaves that tickle and tease,
They dance in the soft, gentle breeze.
Roots tangled in tales of delight,
Under the moon and soft starlight.

A sunflower wearing a hat,
Wonders if it might be a cat.
What fun if they could speak,
Would they giggle or simply squeak?

So come join this leafy jest,
Where every sprout is a fest.
In a world where odd things bloom,
Laughter dances, chasing gloom.

Twines of Tranquility

On the fence, a plant sprawls wide,
With tendrils that gently glide.
Climbing high, oh what a sight!
It tickles the clouds with delight.

Chasing sunlight, a sneaky sprout,
Peeking in at a picnic, no doubt.
It sends a wink to the ants below,
"Care for a ride? Come on, let's go!"

Bouncing leaves, they join in a race,
Poking fun with a leafy grace.
One takes a nap on a sunlit stone,
While others giggle at a garden grown.

Such joy in their playful spree,
Nature's own special comedy.
In this embrace, life intertwines,
With chuckles in every line.

Flourishing Pathways

Down the path where shadows play,
A twisty plant shows the way.
Creeping around with a grin,
Whispers secrets on the wind.

It winks at flowers, bright and bold,
Sharing stories, both new and old.
A daisy chuckles with a sigh,
"Watch out! Here comes a butterfly!"

Twisting round every nook and cranny,
Creating mischief, oh so uncanny.
A little frog hops, looks surprised,
At the antics that are well disguised.

So wander here, where laughter grows,
In the company of amigos.
Each twist and turn, a tale divine,
In this garden, everything's fine!

The Aisles of Arbor

In a forest, a funny scene,
Branches play hide and seek, quite keen.
"Catch me if you can!" they shout,
As squirrels dash in and out.

Beneath the boughs, a party brews,
With critters sharing silly news.
A raccoon wearing a tiny tie,
Juggles acorns, oh my, oh my!

Each tree has its own quirky flair,
Telling jokes in the cool, fresh air.
Leaves laughing till they turn red,
A comedy waiting to be spread.

In the aisles of this wooded show,
Where nature dances, and giggles flow.
Every corner, a chance to cheer,
With laughter blossoming everywhere.

Tangled Threads of Time and Space

In the garden of twists, the time's on a spree,
Rabbits wear clocks, sipping tea with the bee.
Mice in top hats on a wild merry-go-round,
Dance with the shadows, where silliness found.

A snail on a skateboard races the breeze,
While turtles do tango beneath the tall trees.
Upside-down dreams hang like socks on a line,
Wobbling giggles, oh what a fun time!

The frogs wear this hats, one's plaid and the other,
Claims he's the prince—oh, don't tell his mother!
Laughter erupts from the leaves in a whirl,
As squirrels steal bandanas and dance with a twirl.

In the depths of the night, all creatures convene,
With wisecracks and puns, they're quirky and keen.
Between time and space, where the odd rules the day,
They tango through jokes in a whimsical way.

Blossoms of Tomorrow in Yesterday's Garden

In yesterday's garden, the daisies confide,
That future's a riddle and time's on a slide.
The tulips tell tales of a rain-dancing cow,
While sunflowers giggle, 'We don't know how!'

The roses debate if they should wear blue,
While weeds throw a party, in sneakers, who knew?
With laughter and petals they twirl in a game,
As bees buzz around with a joke that's the same.

The daisies split jokes with the ferns standing tall,
While carrots insist they can sing with a ball.
They hop on their roots, with a wink and a nod,
Creating a scene that's amusingly odd.

Each blossom a character with laughter to share,
As worms crack some barb jokes, without any care.
In tomorrow's bright light, they dance on the ground,
With petals and puns, in joy they are found.

The Hidden Currents of Green Dreams

Under leafy covers, the whispers reside,
Where dreams take a bath in the river's wild ride.
The dandelions giggle, their wishes take flight,
As slippers of frogs skip along through the night.

The fish in the pond wear their best silver ties,
While crickets recite their most brilliant of lies.
They host a great shindig amid snickers and glee,
With stars as the guests and the moon as the key.

The cattails are telling their tales of delight,
Each flick of a leaf brings a chuckle in flight.
In streams made of giggles, the laughter can flow,
As shadows do cartwheels in the twilight glow.

In a world dressed in green, where dreams softly churn,
A fest of the silly, with joy they discern.
The hidden currents, full of humor and cheer,
Guide dreams to the surface, for all friends to hear.

Lush Paths of Resilience

In the lushest of paths, where the laughter takes hold,
Bouncing bunnies boast of the stories they've told.
The flowers play hopscotch beneath the tall oak,
While bushes crack jokes, making all of them choke.

Squirrels tell tales of great acorn heists,
While hedgehogs spin yarns, serving biscuits with feasts.
With resilience wrapped in a joyful embrace,
Every twist in the path has a smile on its face.

The sunflowers stand guard, with echoes of cheer,
As daisies compose with a symphony near.
In this vibrant parade of giggles and glee,
All creatures take joy in their sprightly esprit.

So wander these paths where the silly unfurls,
In resilient steps, let your laughter be twirls.
For every small whimsy, there's strength to be found,
In the lush fields of fun, where humor is sound.

Sigils of the Soil

In gardens deep where the weeds laugh,
A carrot hides, it's on the wrong path.
The tomatoes gossip beneath wide leaves,
As ladybugs dance, tossing out thieves.

The worms have meetings, all quite absurd,
Discussing plans without a single word.
With beetles wearing hats so fine,
Who knew the soil could throw such a line?

A pumpkin declared he'd roll to fame,
But tripped on roots, oh, what a shame!
The lettuce chuckles, plucking a joke,
As radishes blush from the farmer's poke.

So dig and sow, let laughter be heard,
Each plant a comedy, quite absurd.
With dirt on our hands, and smiles to grow,
The garden is lively, with plenty to show.

The Green Mosaic

Chlorophyll hats on heads so spry,
Cabbages prancing beneath the blue sky.
Carrots in chitchat, how they delight,
Sharing their stories by soft moonlight.

The flowers wear ties, so dapper and bright,
Petunias and pansies, a colorful sight.
With whispers of secrets caught in the breeze,
Sunflowers gossip, if you please, if you please!

A sprout waddles in a dance so round,
While rhubarb warns, "Watch where you bound!"
Their laughter echoes among the greens,
In this patch of joy, anything leans.

So join this ball, whirls of delight,
A plant party happening every night.
With roots in the earth, and laughter to share,
Nature's jesters, if you dare, if you dare!

Patterns of the Wild

In the forest, the ferns do a jig,
Squirrels debate if they should wear a wig.
The owls are wise, with spectacles round,
Who knew wisdom could also be found?

Raccoons in masks plan midnight affairs,
While bunnies bounce tales of silly snares.
The brook is chuckling with pebbles so shy,
And frogs are at karaoke, Oh my, oh my!

The trees sway gently, playing a tune,
Their branches a piano, hums with the moon.
With all of nature's quirks on parade,
Who needs a circus when life's this cascade?

So wander and wonder, let giggles unwind,
In the patterns of wild, new joy you will find.
With each critter's jest, and a light-hearted twist,
You'll laugh with the creatures, it's too good to miss!

Nature's Embrace

A hedgehog grins, in a cozy embrace,
With butterflies dancing, we join the chase.
The daisies are laughing, their petals a-flutter,
Whispering secrets, "Here comes the nutter!"

The rabbits wear sneakers, ready to race,
While hedges gossip of the new squirrel's face.
The sunbeams tickle the leaves up high,
As the ants parade by, waving, oh my!

A fox wears glasses, too cool for a hound,
With fashion so stellar, he's turning around.
The bees are the DJs, spinning their tunes,
Even the crickets join in for some swoons.

So step into nature, leave worries behind,
Embrace the silliness, let laughter unwind.
In each leafy corner, in every soft sound,
Nature's embrace wraps us safe and profound.

The Green Path

In a garden of sprightly green,
The twists and the turns are quite seen.
I tripped on a root, what a sight!
A tumble of clumsy delight!

The hedges are talking, I swear!
With whispers of secrets to share.
But plants keep their gossip so sly,
With leaves spinning tales as they sigh.

A wanderer lost in the maze,
Confused by the sun's dappled rays.
I danced with a shrub, much to my glee,
It laughed as it tangled with me!

So stroll on the path, but beware!
The plants have a sense of fair flair.
With every twist, there's a giggle there,
In nature's embrace, all burdens will clear!

Silken Shadows

Under the cover of leafy twirls,
A game of peek-a-boo unfurls.
The shadows giggle, oh so sly,
As I tiptoe past, watch me fly!

Creeping along with cat-like grace,
I trip over roots, what a chase!
The sunbeams dance, play tricks on me,
A slapstick comedy, can't you see?

The leaves rustle, they're laughing too,
As I bounce from a branch with a view.
Coated in laughter, I rise so bold,
In nature's jest, life never gets old!

With every sculpted shadow I see,
The world becomes funnier than it should be.
So let's all find joy in the playful play,
In these silken shadows, come join the fray!

The Allure of Climbing

Up high on a branch, I do sway,
Chasing the breeze, what a display!
Each step feels wobbly, a comedic fall,
But laughter erupts, I'm having a ball!

With every grasp, my grip gets tight,
The squirrels mock me, what a sight!
They chatter away while I'm stuck up here,
Conquering branches, fueled by cheer.

Around me, the leaves and the sky collide,
In this merry dance, I take pride.
Each climb leads to ticklish heights,
With giggles igniting my flighty sights!

So here's to the climb, full of blunders,
Falling for fun and nature's wonders.
With every stumble and every climb,
I find joy in the silliness—it's simply sublime!

Timeless Tangents

In a garden of quirks beneath my feet,
I discover the joy that's quite the treat.
Each twist and turn, a laugh to behold,
As stories unfold from the roots, ages old.

With tendrils of joy and curls of delight,
I frolic through paths from morning 'til night.
The colors all blend in a nonsensical way,
As laughter erupts, come join the play!

The flowers tease me with scents so bizarre,
While dancing around like they're stars on a bar.
I trip over daisies, they snicker and cheer,
In this timeless adventure, I've nothing to fear!

So embrace the tangents, the wild and the free,
In every odd nook, there's fun waiting for thee.
With humor entwined in the petals and dew,
Life's a hilarious journey, come see it anew!

Blossoms of Forgotten Memories

In a garden of laughter, flowers weep,
Antics of bees, buzzing secrets to keep.
Silly gnomes trip over tangled roots,
While daisies giggle in polka-dot suits.

A snail slips by, wearing a hat too bright,
Waving at worms in a wiggly flight.
Old roses reminisce about days long gone,
As clowns on the patio dance till dawn.

Sunflowers whisper sweet, silly tales,
Of how they once chased the bouncy snails.
With petals like confetti, they throw a bash,
For every bad joke, they hoot and they flash!

A breeze brings a chuckle, a tickle of joy,
As we cling to moments, our laughter, oh boy!
With blossoms around us, we twirl and spin,
In the chaos of memories, let fun begin!

The Art of Twining Desires

Ropes of green, laced with wishes untold,
Twists and turns in what we behold.
A squirrel steals acorns, with eyes full of glee,
As dreams twist like tendrils around every tree.

Laughter erupts at a frog's little leap,
Turning shy flowers into hilarious heaps.
The sun peeks through canvas of cheeky vines,
As petals parade in their fanciful lines.

Whimsical whispers float through the air,
Where the clowns get all tangled in roots everywhere.
The art of twining, with folly and flair,
Leaves us all chuckling, without a care.

Comically tangled, we stumble and dance,
Each twist a reminder to always take a chance.
So gather your giggles; let's create a spree,
In the fun of the moment, just be wild and free!

Petals Dancing in the Breeze

Oh, the petals are jitterbugs, dancing in flight,
Swirling and twirling, a humorous sight.
A ladybug giggles while tracing the floor,
As flowers all chuckle, we can't help but roar.

Here comes the poodle on spindly legs,
Trying to join in with the jiggly pegs.
It's a wild jamboree, no rules to obey,
Where petals laugh loudly, come what may!

The wind chimes in with a joke that we share,
While bees do a two-step, full of flair.
Each rustle and ruffle is a song of delight,
As petals keep boogieing deep into night.

With zany antics and bursts of pure joy,
These petals and critters, they'll never annoy.
Let's sway with the breeze and lose all our cares,
In this party of petals, joy blossoms and flares!

Chasing Light through Leafy Canopies

Beneath the green ceiling, shadows play tricks,
Where squirrels do pirouettes, acrobatic kicks.
The sunbeams burst forth like firework streams,
Chasing the light through the forest of dreams.

Leaves giggle gently, tickled by air,
As whispering branches tease tales of despair.
But laughter erupts, a comical cheer,
From critters all wondering when spring will appear.

A rabbit in sunglasses hops to the beat,
While butterfly buddies shuffle their feet.
And up in the branches, the tall tales unwind,
As shadows team up in the most crazy kind.

In this canopy's charm, life dances with glee,
Each shimmer of sunshine, a wink, a decree.
So come join the chase, let nothing confound,
In the playful wild woods, pure joy is unbound!

Entangled Elegance

In a garden where plants do sway,
It's hard to tell night from day.
A twist and turn, a tangle tight,
Who stepped on whom? Oh, what a sight!

The daisies giggle, the roses snicker,
While ivy climbs, thinking it's slicker.
A sunflower drops its hat in dismay,
"Who knew this fence would ruin my play?"

Yet amid this chaos, joy is found,
In every loop, and every mound.
Who knew a weed could wear a crown,
In this floral circus, no one frowns!

So gather 'round, and laugh with glee,
Nature's mischief is quite the spree.
For in this garden, what's clear as day,
Is tangled fun is the only way!

Emerald Embrace

In a patch of green, where chaos reigns,
The grass said, "Can't we loosen the chains?"
A hedge hog tumbled, oh what a sound,
As snails held a race to see who's the round.

There's laughter flowering, petal by petal,
As weeds tell tales, but never settle.
A bush whispered secrets, the daisies blushed,
While the shy lilac simply hushed.

The ferns flailed arms with a wavy cheer,
While nearby thorns hid their own sneer.
"Who will trip?" a daisy did state,
"Place your bets, we'll just wait and celebrate!"

So here in jade, the banter flows,
Life's little quirks, everybody knows.
An emerald gathering, all in a bunch,
Where every leaf enjoys a silly lunch!

Veins of the Earth

Beneath the soil where laughter grows,
The roots gather tales, as everyone knows.
A carrot chuckled, a beet turned red,
As worms told jokes about what they fed!

A radish said, "I'm feeling quite snappy!"
As peas in pods got all grumpy and flappy.
"I can't stand much longer in this tight spot!"
While pumpkins debated who's looking hot.

With every poke, and every squirm,
The ground erupted, oh what a term!
Nature's laughter hums low and deep,
In these veins, surprise secrets creep.

So come on down, enjoy the mirth,
In the cheeky layers of the Earth.
For there's giggles stashed in every clod,
A rollicking riot, from humble pod.

Flourishing Fables

In a land where greens take a twisty note,
The flowers tell tales, in laughter they gloat.
"I once was shy, but grew to be bold!"
Cried the bush, as it proudly told.

The daisies danced in whimsical cheer,
"Let's make a party, clear your fear!"
The petals whirled, in joyful blend,
While thorns around, plotting to fend.

A fickle vine shouted, "Look at me!"
As it swung from a tree, what a sight to see!
The roses rolled, in fits and giggles,
"This is the place for funky wiggles!"

So join the fun, in this playful plot,
Where every leaf has a story, a thought.
In the land of blooms, laughter's a staple,
With every flourish, a giggly fable!

Shadows of Serenity

In the garden where grapes hang low,
A bird hopped by, stealing the show.
With a wiggle and wobble, it danced so free,
Chasing its shadow, oh what a spree!

The sun peeked out from clouds so gray,
It threw confetti in a modern way.
Buzzing bees laughed, in their tiny flight,
They'd sip on nectar, a comical sight!

A squirrel found acorns, hidden with flair,
Juggling his treasures, without a care.
He slipped on a leaf, tumbled with glee,
A nature's clown, wild and carefree!

Laughter echoed through branches above,
A frog croaked jokes, all in good love.
With each little croak, the laughter grew,
In this lively nook, joy always flew!

The Essence of Entanglement

In a twisty path, where roots intertwine,
A gnome made a deal with a bottle of wine.
He slurred his words, with a twinkle in eye,
"Who needs a map? Just drink and fly!"

A cat with a hat, so charming and sly,
Joined in the party, as the fireflies cry.
He tangled with vines, thinking it grand,
But fell on his face with a slap of the hand!

The moon rolled out, wearing a smug grin,
"Let's dance on the lawn, let the fun begin!"
With throngs of odd critters, all in a spin,
One little worm said, "Do I join in?"

A dance-off erupted, with moves quite bizarre,
A turtle in slippers, a fish with a guitar.
They laughed 'till they cried, all tangled like so,
In this silly tangle, the laughter would flow!

Flurries of Flora

In a patch of daisies, a bee wore a hat,
He buzzed like he owned this sweet little spat.
With each tiny buzz, he started a trend,
Even flowers would giggle, and sway like a friend!

A hedgehog in socks just rolled through the blooms,
Spreading soft petals like fluffy costumes.
He stumbled and tumbled, what a surprise,
As daisies joined in with giggles and sighs!

Butterflies fluttered, a cheeky display,
Wearing polka dots, led the dancing ballet.
They twirled in the air, what a sight to behold,
While petals rained down like stories retold!

A rabbit brought snacks, with a hop and a skip,
He juggled his treats, but slipped on a dip.
In flurries of laughter, the party took flight,
Nature's wild fun in the warm golden light!

Rhythms of Rustling

In the whispers of leaves, secrets unfold,
A chubby raccoon dove, brave and bold.
He rummaged around, with a snicker and chuckle,
Found a bright donut, and let out a rumble!

Crickets played music, in harmony lit,
With a beat of the drums, the fireflies lit.
The breeze took the stage, swaying along,
As the creatures all clapped to the rustle-song!

Down in the bushes, a hedgehog did prance,
He danced with the wind, in a mystical trance.
He slipped on a twig, went tumbling fast,
But laughed off the tumble, a riotous blast!

So under the moon, they boogied all night,
With the rustling rhythms, everything felt right.
In joyous momentum, they twirled and spun,
This kingdom of laughter was never outdone!

The Color of Connection

In a garden where laughter sways,
Colors clash in silly ways.
A bluebird dons a polka dot tie,
While sunflowers giggle as bees buzz by.

The daisies dance, they trip and fall,
With petals bright, they have a ball.
A rainbow's charm, a playful tease,
In this field of chatter, grown by ease.

When colors mingle, oh what a sight,
A jester's hat on the moon so bright.
With every hue, a tale unfolds,
In this world of color, life never gets old.

So let's hold hands in this riotous spree,
With blossoms laughing, wild and free.
In the palette of joy, let's play our part,
With every burst of color, let's share a heart!

Trails of Time

On rolling roads where giggles tread,
Each twisty turn's a tale that's spread.
The clock does tick, but who can tell,
If the past is a story or just a spell?

A squirrel zips by on a vintage bike,
With acorns stacked, what a sight!
Tick-tock, the trees lean in to hear,
The whispers of laughter floating near.

A pathway paved with jests and dreams,
The sun plays tricks with its golden beams.
Rabbits leap with a cheeky flair,
On this trail, time dances without a care.

So let's wander where time's a prank,
Through meadows lush and the riverbank.
For in the trails where we retreat,
We find the joys that can't be beat!

The Fabric of Flora

In threads of leaves and petals fine,
Nature stitches a quilt divine.
With stitches bright and patterns bold,
A tapestry of tales is told.

The cornflowers weave a joke so sly,
As the roses blush in the evening sky.
With every patch, a giggle sewn,
In this fabric of flora, joy is grown.

A patchwork party, a playful spree,
With daisies chattering in harmony.
Sewing sunshine, trimming gloom,
In this garden, laughter blooms.

So wrap yourself in nature's thread,
Where joy is sown and worries shed.
In this fabric, every seam,
Is stitched with love, and laughter gleams!

Enchanted Twists

In a jungle where the vines take flight,
Twisting around with all their might.
A monkey swings with a cheeky grin,
In this enchanted mess of joy within!

Each curl and flip is a funny feat,
As flowers poke through, looking sweet.
The laughter echoes from tree to tree,
In this tangled dance, wild and free.

A maze of green with surprises bright,
Where spiders spin webs with pure delight.
Bumblebees buzz in a merry chase,
In this twisting world, there's ample space.

Let's twirl and swirl through this wild ride,
With every turn, we find joy inside.
For in the twists where magic plays,
Laughter lives in curious ways!

Veiled Trails

Among the leaves, they twist and twine,
A maze of green, it's quite divine.
They play a game of hide and seek,
With sneaky curls and branches sleek.

A squirrel giggles as it darts,
Through tangled paths of leafy arts.
The sun peeks in, the shadows dance,
Each wiggle leads to a new chance.

The ground is soft, the air is sweet,
But watch your step, or you'll face defeat!
For every trip, there's a surprise,
A tickling leaf or bug that flies.

So wander through this leafy maze,
Where laughter echoes, sunlight plays.
With every step, fun twists uncoil,
In this green world, good times unspoiled.

Nature's Canvas

The branches paint with strokes so bold,
Each twist a tale that must be told.
With every curl, the laughter grows,
A world of fun that ebbs and flows.

A robin hops on a leafy perch,
While elders sigh in leafy lurch.
A painter's dream set in the sun,
Where humor blooms, and joy's begun.

An acorn tumbles from its place,
Like nature's way of making space.
Each leaf a jester in disguise,
With silly shapes that make you rise.

So wander wide, let laughter ring,
In every twist, the joy they bring.
Nature's art is never still,
In this bright realm, we find our thrill.

Emerald Harmony

In tangled webs of emerald hue,
The giggles play hide-and-seek too.
A chubby frog leaps with great glee,
As it splashes loud, what a sight to see!

Laughter cloaks the winding path,
As sunlight spills the bright aftermath.
With every turn, a tale unfolds,
Of silly bugs and mischief bold.

The crickets chirp a funny song,
Their rhythm keeps the day prolonged.
While flowers sway as if in jest,
Inviting all to join the fest.

In this vibrant dance, we find delight,
Nature's humor on full flight.
So take my hand, let's skip along,
In this green world, where we belong!

Spirals in the Shade

In very odd and twirly ways,
The leaves perform their funny plays.
A lazy bee takes center stage,
Buzzing round like it's the age!

The shadows wiggle, stretch, and sway,
As if to wish the light away.
A rabbit hops, with ears that flop,
In this wild show, it's hard to stop!

The petals giggle with colors bright,
As whispers of mischief take flight.
With every twist, a chuckle blooms,
Dancing shadows in vibrant rooms.

So come and take this winding ride,
Where joy and fun are there to guide.
In spirals deep, our laughter weaves,
A merry tale among the leaves.

Climbing Above the Shadows

In a garden where socks might hang low,
I tripped on a root, oh no, whoa!
Laughter erupted, the birds sang along,
While I danced with a leaf like it knew a song.

The sun peeked through branches, a playful thief,
Spreading giggles like flowers, oh what a relief!
I climbed up the wall, thought I was quite spry,
But slipped on a banana, and up I did fly!

The squirrels all chuckled, the rabbits gave cheer,
As I rolled down the hill, oh dear, oh dear!
With mud on my face and joy in my heart,
I climbed above shadows, now that's art!

So if you find laughter in nature's wild dance,
Just join in the fun, give your dreams a chance!
For climbing above with a giggle and twist,
Is a life full of joy that should never be missed!

Nature's Embrace: A Tangle of Dreams

In the whispering leaves, dreams come alive,
A squirrel in a tutu decided to jive.
The branches all chuckled as I passed them by,
"Join in the fun!" they would say, oh my!

With flowers as hats, we danced round and round,
While bees buzzed solo, a funny lil' sound.
The babbling brook laughed at my goofy face,
Nature's embrace felt like a warm, sweet place.

Then came the wind with a mischievous grin,
Twirling my hair, oh where to begin?
I chased after clouds that looked like a snack,
But they giggled and floated, "You'll never catch back!"

In this tangle of laughter, dreams start to bloom,
Where nature's sweet humor chases away gloom.
So frolic and play in the wild, wild scene,
For life is a dance, and we're all part of the dream!

Soft Footsteps on Fertile Ground

Tiptoeing softly on fertile ground,
I stumbled on carrots, oh, what was that sound?
They giggled and wiggled, a veggie ballet,
"Come join the dance, don't just stroll away!"

The daisies were gossiping, "Who wore it best?"
While my footwear apparently failed the test.
With roots tangled up like a silly parade,
I danced with the weeds, unafraid, unafraid!

The puddles winked up with a cheeky delight,
As I splashed and I laughed in the morning light.
The sun peeked down, saying, "Play for a while,
Make friends with the soil, give the Earth a smile!"

So dance with the dirt, let your heart take flight,
For soft footsteps make laughter the truest delight.
In gardens where giggles take root and abound,
Life blooms with a joy that is profoundly found!

The Language of Climbing Hearts

Up the trees where heartstrings are tied,
I met a wise owl, wearing a grin wide.
"Climb up!" he hooted, "Let's take a great trip,
While I tell you stories, just don't let it slip!"

With branches like fingers, we reached for the sky,
While petals were laughing, "Oh my, oh my!"
The rivers below streamed chuckles so bright,
As we danced from the day into starry night.

"What's the secret?" I asked with a glimmer of hope,
The owl just winked, "It's a slippery slope!
Just climb with your spirit, let laughter unfold,
For the language of love can't be bought or sold."

So up we went, hearts soaring so high,
With giggles and whispers drifting through the sky.
Climbing together, with joy as our art,
In the beautiful symphony of climbing hearts!

Intertwined Paths

Two silly twists, they dance so bright,
A grape and a leaf, a wobbly sight.
They tangle and giggle, a playful spree,
As bugs cheer them on, it's quite a jubilee.

With every loop, they share their tales,
Of berry dreams and wind-blown gales.
They laugh at the clouds that float on by,
And wave to the bees that busily fly.

The sun sets low, they take a bow,
A chortling pair, oh how they wow!
Embraced in the night with sparkles to see,
Who knew plants could act so carefree?

As shadows stretch long, they play hide and seek,
In this leafy tale—no room for the meek.
The roots may be grounded, but hearts take flight,
Intertwined paths, what a comical sight!

Roots of Tomorrow

Beneath the soil, they wriggle and squirm,
Two roots having fun, quite the little worm.
They tickle the ground with jokes that they trade,
And cause tiny plants to laugh and cascade.

A duel of depth, who'll grow the most?
One roots for pizza, the other for toast!
Together they giggle, in muck they delight,
While dreaming of futures, oh, what a sight!

They wiggle and wriggle, a rooty ballet,
Spreading their laughter in the great green ballet.
Oh, the stories they plant for the sproutlings to see,
Of roots in the soil, sharing glee and esprit!

When springtime arrives, they'll pop up with flair,
The roots of tomorrow, in sunlight so rare.
They'll share their adventures, each twist and each bend,
In this silly world, where laughter won't end!

Cascading Shadows

Under the leaves, shadows flicker and sway,
A comedic dance in the warm light of day.
They skip and they slide, much to their delight,
These shadows have secrets, all hidden from sight.

With a chuckle and grin, they stretch, then they fold,
Stories of mischief are just waiting to be told.
A crabby old snail with a top hat appears,
And joins in their laughter, shedding all fears.

As night starts to fall, they morph and they play,
Casting silly shapes in their own shadow ballet.
They giggle and wiggle, oh what a show,
Each twist a delight, most amusing to know!

But as dawn starts to break, they whisper goodbyes,
Hiding their laughs in the brightening skies.
In the hush of the morn, they await the next night,
These cascading shadows, a whimsical sight!

Secrets in Sunlight

Beneath the warm rays, secrets do hum,
A tomato and basil, both feeling quite dumb.
They whisper and giggle, what mischief to choose,
As daisies lean in, eager for news.

With sunlight as ink, they mockingly weave,
Tales of the garden, it's hard to believe!
They conjure up laughter, with vines in a twist,
Each story a seed, that simply can't miss.

The air filled with chuckles, oh what a scene,
A parsley joins in, gets up on the green.
Together they plot how to prank the old fence,
In silly camaraderie, they build their suspense.

As evening approaches, they quiet their spree,
Each leaf tucked in tight, tucked safe as can be.
With secrets in sunlight, their mission stays bright,
The plants in the garden, keep laughter in sight!

The Sway of Nature's Serenade

In gardens where the laughter flows,
A twisty dance from roots to toes.
The sunbeams tickle leaves up high,
While pollen parties make us sigh.

The blooms are wearing hats askew,
And buzzing bees just joined the queue.
They cha-cha on their pollen spree,
And giggle at the dogwood tree.

The willow sways with silly grace,
While critters race to win the chase.
A snail says, "I'm just on a roll!"
While frogs leap past, they're on a stroll.

Oh, nature's jesters, full of cheer,
With every wiggle, laugh, and leer.
In verdant realms where fun is found,
The earth spins round with joy abound.

Enchanted Boundaries of Growth

In tangled realms where laughter grows,
The plants wear socks, and grass still glows.
A dapper mushroom hats the scene,
While daisies dance in shades of green.

The fence that holds these mischiefs tight,
Is painted blue and sparkles bright.
With every twist, they play their part,
In this wild world, oh, where's the start?

A squirrel juggles acorns high,
While wayward petals drift and fly.
The fence post winks, its job is clear,
To house the giggles, far and near.

Oh, how they play within this space,
With snickers sprouting all over the place.
And as the sun bids day goodbye,
The shadows laugh and wave, oh my!

Tendrils of Time

In spiraled twists of leafy lore,
The clock ticks funny at the core.
With every hour, the tendrils tease,
As flowers giggle in the breeze.

A creeping fig climbs up the wall,
It glances back, "I'm having a ball!"
The tulips tumble in a spree,
As time forgets to count, you see.

With each tick-tock, a vine does stretch,
Chasing shadows, no need to etch.
A butterfly dons its finest dress,
While the daisies all just dance in jest.

Oh, tendrils twist with joyous vows,
As nature's clock hands dance, just wow!
In every curl, a jest to find,
A playful trick, a love entwined.

Whispering Green

In whispers soft, the leaves confide,
A secret world where giggles hide.
The grass blades plot a sunny prank,
As daisies laugh in bright old rank.

The ivy climbs with sneaky grace,
And tickles trees in their embrace.
The garden holds its breath, in glee,
As fun erupts from every spree.

A breezy voice sings sweet and low,
While chasing shadows, to and fro.
The sunlight twinkles, cheers aloud,
As butterflies form a silly crowd.

Oh, whispering green, your jokes are grand,
With frolicsome vines that take a stand.
In every corner, joy's unveiled,
Where silly secrets have prevailed.

www.ingramcontent.com/pod-product-compliance
Lightning Source LLC
Chambersburg PA
CBHW051647160426
43209CB00004B/824